SITTING

Sitting

A Guide to Good Meditation Posture

Kamalashila

Windhorse Publications

Published by Windhorse Publications
Unit 1-316 The Custard Factory
Gibb Street
Birmingham
B9 4AA

Printed by Colbourne & Underwood
2 Lower Trinity Street
Birmingham, B9 4AG

Cover photograph by Bruce Rae
Cover design by Dhammarati

ISBN 0 904766 37 3

Contents

Introduction

Meditation is the direct method of spiritual development. It is the most direct method Buddhism has to offer for helping us develop higher human qualities. It is 'direct' because when we meditate we work directly with—and on—the mind itself, transforming distraction into concentration, negative emotions into positive ones.

There are of course many 'indirect' methods of spiritual development. These include the practice of generosity and kindness to others, taking up a physical discipline such as Hatha Yoga or T'ai Chi, broadening one's outlook through study, an active involvement in the arts, or even, quite simply, the adoption of a healthy, regular lifestyle.

While the direct method of meditation has a special kind of effectiveness, the indirect methods are extremely important. Nobody can meditate all the time, and what we do with the major part of our lives—when we are not meditating—is bound to affect our mental states and thus our spiritual progress too. So it is vital to practise some of these indirect methods, for otherwise we will find that the states of mind we cultivate during meditation practice are weakened or even destroyed during the intervals following each session. To summarize, if genuine progress is to be made, meditation practice is not enough by itself. It needs support.

This brings us to the main theme of this booklet. For even while we are practising meditation, the mental effort involved requires some simple physical support: it requires a good meditation posture.

If you meditate regularly, there is a good chance that you will have had the experience of trying to do so whilst being distracted by aches and pains in the back or in the legs. At such times it is clear that working solely with the mind is not enough. To a certain extent one can try to ignore these complaints—treating them as just another hindrance to

concentration. This approach can work if you are alread
very good at meditation. If you are able to get into th
dhyanas (states of higher meditative absorption, in which
one experiences great clarity and enjoyment), physical dis
comfort will recede far into the background and cease t
matter. But more usually the physical discomfort demand
our attention long before we have been able to get properl
concentrated, and unless we do something about it it wil
nag at us until we are unable to carry on with ou
practice.

Although there is no special reason why someone jus
embarking on the practice of meditation should not sit on
firm chair, most people prefer to try sitting on the floo
either cross-legged, or kneeling astride a cushion or lov
stool. Nevertheless, most Westerners tend to find thi
rather difficult at first. In the kind of beginners' meditatio
classes being offered at most public Buddhist centres, ther
is rarely enough time to talk about posture in anything bu
a rudimentary, generalized fashion. Then, if no specificall
personal instruction is sought, the new meditator ma
develop a series of bad postural habits. It is very easy, fo
example, to adopt a sitting position which gives temporar
support, but which is physiologically incorrect, and ever
harmful. Physical problems that arise out of such ba
habits can be very difficult to correct.

The remedy is, first and foremost, to seek some persona
instruction. But the contents of this booklet may also hel
those new to meditation to avoid some of the worse pro
blems altogether. They will also serve as a 'trouble
shooting guide' for more experienced meditators. Thes
days, physical posture and deportment are not especiall
fashionable topics. Although the benefits of fitness seem t
be generally acknowledged, some of the subtler aspects o
physical health could perhaps be appreciated more. On
such aspect is the relationship between physical and men
tal health, on the one hand, and physical posture—or it
kinetic counterpart, deportment,—on the other.

Anyone trying to practise mindfulness (Pali: *sati,* consciou
awareness and recollection) will be aware of this connec

tion. For Buddhism, mindfulness is the central axis—the growing point—of all human development, and it is towards the physical body that mindfulness is first to be directed. Buddhism defines four 'foundations' for mindfulness, which together sum up our experience of ourselves. Awareness of the body and its movements is the first and most basic; the three others are mental, and can be summarized (very simply) as awareness of: feeling (the passive experience of pleasure or pain whether weak or strong), the emotions (our active responses to feeling), and thoughts. Thus, for Buddhism, awareness of the body is the indispensable basis and starting point for the awareness, and for the higher development, of the whole person.

In *A Survey of Buddhism*, Sangharakshita writes of the importance of awareness of the body. Quoting J. Evola's observation on mindfulness, that '. . . by following such a path a man transforms himself into . . . a figure pervaded by composedness, decorum and dignity', he adds:

'Bodily composure, though itself the product of a certain mental attitude, turns round as it were and, reacting on the mind, produces an even deeper quietude of spirit than before. It should moreover be noted that through the practice of mindfulness and self-possession the most trivial occasions of life are invested with a halo of sanctity. Eating, drinking, and dressing, the processes of excretion and urination even, are transformed from hindrances into helps to concentration; from interruptions of the spiritual life they become its continuation under another form.'[1]

So mindfulness is a state of near-meditation. To be mindful is to be in a perceptibly higher state of being and consciousness. If we try to be more clearly conscious of our body and mind outside of our formal sitting practice, we will find our meditation becoming far easier, because we will have become accustomed to the process of constant self-monitoring and the honesty it requires. If we try to 'switch on' some self-awareness only for the time when we are

[1] Sangharakshita, *A Survey of Buddhism*, (Windhorse, 1993) p.174

meditating, much of the session will be taken up with har
preliminary work. The more preparation we do, the le
resistance will arise from the unconscious mind.

We cannot meditate with our minds alone, unaided. In
sense, body and mind make up one unit. Their function
are mutually interdependent, always affecting one anothe
mental actions can produce physical results, and vice vers
Bodily awareness produces a certain concentratio
of mind: a concentrated mind is actually physicall
pleasurable.

Mindfulness of the body helps develop good physical pos
ture. In meditation, good posture helps us to engage wit
the practice. Posture thus affects our mental state, and so
can be utilized as a means of working in meditation. Thi
booklet will explain what good meditation posture is, an
how to put our new understanding into practice.

What Makes a Good Meditation Posture

A good meditation posture is one which provides the best possible position for physical relaxation and concentration of mind. In such a position we should ideally be able to sit completely still for as long as we wish. In order to relax fully, the bodily system must be able to function with a minimum expenditure of energy, the heart should be at its quietest, and the lungs unrestricted so that the intake and outflow of air is correspondingly quiet and natural. At the same time, the mind is to be alert and poised. Thus it is best if the body is kept upright rather than lying down. If the weight of the trunk is balanced vertically above the seat, a minimum of muscular effort is required to support it. Sitting is therefore the best position, for when we sit the strain upon our limbs is at a minimum. As far as possible each arm and leg should be symmetrically balanced with its partner, so that there is no tension anywhere. Meditation certainly can be practised sitting in an upright chair, but when possible it is better performed sitting on the floor with the legs drawn close to the trunk. This further minimizes the expenditure of energy on muscle support and blood circulation.

If we consciously sit in a posture which minimizes strain, and in which we can also be alert, we will find it much easier to concentrate. This is the basic principle of the posture work in the more detailed sections which follow.

How Problems With Posture Arise

The problem that arises most often when we sit in one position for long periods of time is physical discomfort. Sooner or later our knees start aching, or our back or neck develops a twinge. At first, these may have something to do with lack of practice—we are just not used to sitting still on the floor. But generally, the main cause of aches and pains is tension: muscles are tight and stretched when they should be relaxed. Such tension could be due to an unbalanced pos-

ture which places too much pressure on certain areas, w
might simply be cold, or the tension might have its roots i
our mental and emotional state.

So before examining the way we actually sit, we shoul
perhaps take note of the factors outside of meditatio
which might cause tensions. For example, let's consider th
case of someone who is round-shouldered and closed
chested. This physical stance quite likely has an emotiona
cause: perhaps the person has a poor self-image and lack
confidence. To make things worse, the habit of holding th
body in this constricting position may have confirmed th
emotion even more, dulling energy, and making the per
son 'in-turned', over-subjective. Thus it is that poor postur
can serve both as a cause and as a result of negativ
emotions. By simply standing more upright, by not hunch
ing our shoulders, by relaxing our head and neck, most o
us will find that we can greatly improve our menta
state!

But there can also be straightforward physical reasons fo
bad posture. If there is a weakness in one part of the body, i
will cause extra strain elsewhere. That strain will eithe
weaken the affected part, or extra musculature will develo
to cope with it. If extra muscle does develop in compensa
tion, the original weakness may be fixed, and furthe
degeneration may take place. In this way a pattern of ten
sion and compensatory reaction is repeated throughou
the body, and thus begins a gradual process of uneven
development. For example, a person with one leg shorte
than the other (which is more common than you migh
think) will have to work the back muscles on one side mor
than the other. In compensation, one shoulder may be held
higher than the other—to adjust for which, the neck and
head will have to be held over to one side. . . . A sligh
deformity such as this can go unnoticed for many years—
until it comes to sitting still for thirty or forty minutes! Very
often, it is not until people start practising meditation tha
their ingrained physical imbalances and difficulties begin
to reveal themselves.

This relationship between body and mind—between emotion and posture—does of course have a positive side. A joyful emotional state will naturally reflect itself in the way we sit, stand, and move. In meditation, a bright meditative state will naturally give rise to an improved sitting posture. As we meditate, as our initial mental chaos clarifies and integrates, our body will begin to feel lighter and more relaxed, the distracting, niggling discomforts will gradually lessen. Then we may find that our back begins to straighten, our chest to open, and our shoulders and arms to relax back. At the very least, we should become aware of the extent to which our present position is restricted and restrictive: a straighter back and an open chest will begin to feel more natural, and we will start to acquire an intuitive understanding of what good .meditation posture could be.

Posture As a Meditation Method

As well as serving as an important basis for physical health and meditation practice, posture can be approached as a sort of meditation method in its own right. Good posture alone can help counteract some of the most common hindrances to meditation. Buddhist tradition specifically speaks of five 'hindrances' (Pali: *nivaranas*). These are, firstly, desire for sense experience, secondly, anger, thirdly, sloth and torpor, fourthly, restlessness and anxiety, and fifthly, doubt.

Let's look for a moment at 'sloth and torpor'. Sometimes either our minds or our bodies, or both, are dull and sleepy, uninterested in meditation. At such times, when we are unlikely to engage with a proper meditation practice and are in fact set to drift away into a spell of undirected daydreaming, we can instead at least decide to spend the meditation session trying to maintain a good posture. Even if our mind is unable to grasp a more subtle meditation object, we can at least make an effort to remain awake and sit correctly. If we can persist in bringing our attention back to the body, checking for arching in the back or slumping— and other points which will be explained later—the hindrance is likely to disperse before the end of the session, and we should be able to move on to a definite meditation technique. But even if this hindrance is extremely strong (as it sometimes can be), and we are not able to meditate properly even after half an hour or forty minutes, nevertheless, by holding it at bay we will have weakened its power over us.

We can also do something about the opposite mental extreme, the hindrance of restlessness and anxiety through concentration on posture. Physical restlessness means that we find it uncomfortable to sit still; similarly the mind, when anxious, cannot become peaceful. One method of counteracting both the mental and physical agitation is quite simply to determine to sit absolutely still. The mind cannot be made to be still, but the body can—if we definitely decide that it is going to be! Then, taking the stillness of the body as the main object of our meditation practice, the restless mind will eventually calm down and be at peace. If the agitation is very strong, this process will probably take some time. But if, without forcing the mind, we persist patiently in stilling the body, we will be successful in the end.

fig. 1 The ideal meditation posture

fig. 2 Dhyana mudra

fig. 3 Side view showing cushions

fig. 4 Side view showing stool

The Ideal Meditation Posture

Any bodily posture which reflects, or conduces to, a higher state of consciousness is known in traditional Eastern terminology as a *mudra*. The ideal meditation mudra is the well known 'full lotus' position. This consists of seven aspects:

1. The legs should be crossed with each foot placed, sole uppermost, upon the thigh of the other leg (i.e. in 'full lotus').

2. The spine should be upright, neither arching backwards nor slumping forwards.

3. The hands should be held in the lap, two or three inches below the navel. The palms both face upwards, one over the other so that the thumb-tips lightly touch. This hand position is called *dhyana mudra* (see fig. 2).

4. The shoulders should be relaxed and drawn somewhat back so as to keep the chest open.

5. The head is balanced on the spine so that there is a slight inclination forwards.

6. The eyes are directed downwards, either lightly closed or half open.

7. The mouth is relaxed, teeth unclenched, lips held lightly together. The tongue just touches the palate behind the teeth.

It must be stressed at once that this is an *ideal* posture. Points 2 to 7 may present little difficulty for most of us, but few Westerners will be able to manage the 'full lotus' leg position, at least to begin with. Luckily, it is not essential to have your legs folded like this, since there are a number of

13

fig. 5 *Sitting on a chair*

fig. 6 *Sitting with back against wall*

fig. 7 *Half lotus*

fig. 8 *One foot on calf*

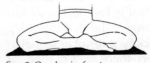

fig. 9 *One leg in front*

other variations which are almost as good. If you look at the diagrams which follow, you should be able to find a position which suits you'for the time being, and then gradually improve upon it.

If you cannot sit cross-legged it is almost as good to sit on a low bench or stool, or on several cushions.

If this is difficult, then try sitting on an ordinary chair as above (note support under chair legs to bring body weight forward).

If the back is weak, then sit supported between the wall and the floor.

Setting Up Your Meditation Posture

It is useful to learn this routine for setting up your posture—then every time you sit down to meditate you will have a systematic way of assessing it. After some practice the routine will become second nature. It may often take no longer than a second or two, whilst at other times you may need to spend more time on it.

Posture setting-up routine:

First: Choose a cushion (or stool, or whatever you use) which seems the right height for you. Then arrange your legs in one of the ways shown (figs. 7, 8, 9). Don't be too concerned for the moment if both of your knees are not on the ground.

Second: Adjust the pelvis so that it is angled fairly vertically. It should not tilt too far backwards or forwards (place hands in front and behind to judge). Become aware of the sensation of the two 'sitting bones' against the seat. The correct position of the pelvis brings these bones into maximum contact with the cushion.

14

fig. 10 Pelvis

Third: Maintaining awareness of the sitting bones, first allow the spinal column to lift lightly and straighten, avoiding rigidity. Take a deep breath or two: this will open the chest and rib-cage. Relax the shoulders and arms, and adjust the hands in the lap so that they are not working against the relaxed-back position of the shoulders and arms. It can be helpful to place a small 'hand-pad' in the lap—it provides a flat surface for the hands, which can then relax more easily. This too will help the shoulders to relax. Place one hand over the other (in *dhyana mudra* or in any other comfortable position).

Fourth: Adjust the head position. Become aware of the neck as an extension of the spine. (If you like, roll it gently backwards and forwards until it feels balanced.) Feel the point where the skull balances upon the spinal column, then let it tilt forwards slightly, so that the gaze is upon the floor a few feet in front of you. Relax the face, jaw, tongue, and throat.

fig. 11 Spine, Chest, Shoulders, Arms

Finally, generally check the whole feeling of the posture, especially the alignment of the trunk from side to side and back to front. If it helps, rock gently from the pelvis until you feel yourself to be in equilibrium. Now (though this can also be done during stage three) check for the two basic sitting faults: slumping forward, or arching backwards. Make any adjustments necessary. Once you are familiar with these faults, you will be able to adjust quickly to very slight variations.

Adjusting Your Posture

(a) Adjusting the seat for height

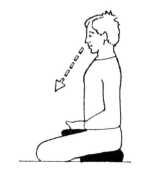

fig. 12 Head

When you set up your posture, even a very slight adjustment in the height of your seat or cushion can make the vital difference. At a certain height you will feel the correct balance of the body, and this awareness will make it easier to adjust the legs and back.

fig. 13 Arching backwards
—Causes pain in lower back.
—Tendency to fall forwards.
—Tendency to extend the tail-bone outwards.

fig. 14 Slumping forward
—Causes pain in neck, shoulders, and upper back.
—Tendency to fall backwards if relaxed.

Too high: If your seat is too high, the upper pelvis moves forwards, and the tail-bone backwards. Then your general tendency is to fall forwards, and for the upper back to arch up and backwards to compensate. This strains the lower back and you will soon begin to feel pains there.

Remedy: If slight, sit up straight. Otherwise, experiment with lower seat.

Too low: If your seat is too low, then the opposite happens—the upper pelvis tends backwards, the tail-bone forwards, and you collapse in the lower back. To stop yourself from falling backwards you tend to slump forwards, closing in your chest at the same time. Painful tension is caused in the neck and shoulders by this awkward positioning.

Remedy: If slight, sit up straight. Otherwise, experiment with higher seat.

Note: To sit up 'straight' does not mean trying to get your spine as straight as a broom handle. It should have a natural curve.

(b) 'Feeling right' does not mean it *is* right!

As we saw in the first section, the entire sitting position needs to be as balanced and symmetrical as possible. Each part of the body is ideally balanced by another, so that there is a minimum amount of strain on the system.

Setting up your posture in the systematic way outlined earlier helps achieve this symmetry and balance. But there is one important problem: you cannot always rely upon whether or not your posture simply *feels* right. Very often, what feels 'right' is merely what we are accustomed to. So when you are placed—by a friend or teacher—in a better posture, it will probably be unfamiliar and may even feel awkward and crooked at first. Your tendency will probably be to gradually move back to the familiar (but incorrect and harmful) posture.

So even if you have practised meditation for a long time, you should not simply accept a feeling of 'rightness' or 'wrongness' in your posture as the only guideline, but try to get an objective assessment. As with many things in life, it is not so easy to see, let alone change, our bad habits! We need personal attention and feed-back. This booklet will not be enough. Ask your friends to take a critical look at your meditation posture, and now and again attend meditation classes and retreats where posture instruction is available.

(c) Pain

One obvious indication of incorrect posture is pain. Certainly there are some aches and pains which are best ignored—minor discomforts which soon pass, feelings of awkwardness, itches, and other irritations. There can be no end to these, and you will never be able to settle down unless you consciously decide to put up with a few of them. As we have already seen, these discomforts are often linked with inner restlessness, an unsettled mind fastening on to, and becoming obsessed by, a relatively minor irritation. By indulging such restlessness, you will not connect with the meditation, and other people meditating with you will also be disturbed. If this is all that is happening, try to recognize the fact, and try to put your attention elsewhere.

fig. 15 Foam or folded blanket for stool

But other pains may well be danger signals. Real pain never arises without a cause. Numbness, for example, ought not to be ignored: it is not good for limbs to become completely numb. Neither should sharp pains, for they almost invariably suggest that something is wrong. I may appear to be stating the obvious, but I have encountered many people who seem to think that meditation practice necessarily involves extreme asceticism. Such people run the risk of doing considerable damage to themselves. Buddhist tradition reminds us that the human body is exceedingly precious and hard to obtain; since it serves as the basis from which we can meditate, gain insight, and even attain Enlightenment, it should be treated with kindness and respect.

Ways To Make Sitting Practice Easier

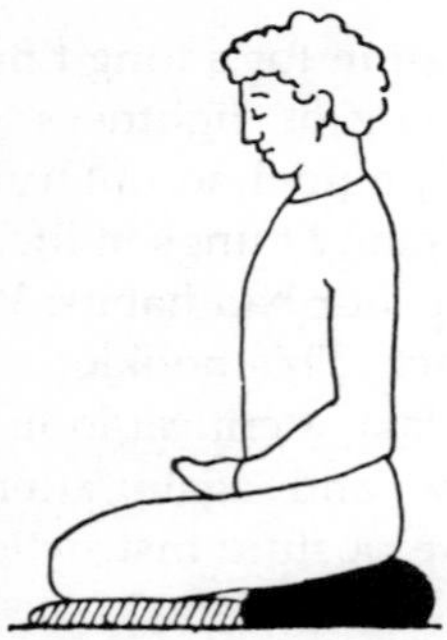

The long term solution to posture difficulties is physical training, and we will soon be looking at a few helpful exercises. In the short term, however, there are a number of ways to make sitting easier:

fig. 16 Pad/blanket to support knees

Except in hot countries, or when you are suffering from the hindrance of sloth and torpor, it is generally helpful to keep the legs and hips warm. Warmth takes the edge off those temporary, inconsequential aches and pains mentioned in the last section. Beneath the legs, whether you are kneeling or cross-legged, you should place a doubled blanket or a foam-rubber pad (though if the foam-rubber extends under the cushion it may make the seat unsteady). This not only insulates the legs but protects the knees. For people who are kneeling it also takes the pressure off the ankles and upper parts of the feet.

fig. 17 Pad under raised knee

In fact, any pressure can be alleviated with cushions and pads. Some people find a small pad—or perhaps a roll of material—helpful if placed behind an aching knee, or so as to cushion an ankle which is pressing into a thigh. If one knee will not touch the ground, a small cushion can be placed there for support.

fig. 18 Blanket for warmth

Finally, uncomfortable hands are a source of distraction. It is therefore very helpful, almost essential, to have some padding beneath them, a flat surface upon which they can be be placed evenly. The position of this hand pad should be high enough to relieve the weight of the arms from the shoulders so that the shoulders can more easily relax down the back, allowing the chest to open freely. See fig.18.

Exercises

(a) Moving 'up' to a better posture

The ideal meditation posture is the cross-legged 'full lotus' because this gives the best balance, the most 'streamlined' feeling, and is (eventually) most comfortable for long periods of sitting. The next best is some other form of cross-legged posture, for example the half-lotus, or a variation of it (see fig. 7). Then come, in order of preference, kneeling with a stool or cushions, and sitting on a chair. Whichever of these positions you use, you could almost certainly be sitting in it better. In the long term you should aim to pass through the positions, aiming for a better one all the time.

Of course, the trouble with such advice is—as I am sure you know—your stiff joints and weak muscles are not used to it: they are going to hold you back. Can anything be done?

(b) How exercise can help

Whatever your age—and however stiff you are—it is possible, over time, to loosen your joints and strengthen your muscles to some extent. Specific exercises do exist. You just have to do them in the right way.

There are many systems of exercise, and within each system there are many exercises. I have therefore collated here a small selection which can be used to work on the parts of the body most affected by meditation practice.

But before you read about—or try—these exercises, I should just make an important introductory remark. The problem with learning exercises from a book is that without a teacher you may do them incorrectly and damage yourself!

If you do not fully understand how to work in a particular exercise, you may become over-confident, push yourself a little too hard, and overdo it. At worst, you could put your back or knees askew, painfully and even permanently. So, while the exercises which follow can certainly be experimented with, be very gentle with yourself. If you decide to take them up seriously, then find someone who can help you to do them correctly.

(c) Four types of exercise

Of all the many different types of exercise, four stand out as being particularly valuable, though each is quite distinct from the others.

Firstly, there is the approach of standard Western 'PT' (Physical Training), which usually involves vigorous movement of selected parts of the body. There are many kinds of PT—some very specific, like weight-lifting, others more general. With PT there is less emphasis upon bodily awareness, but some very effective methods for stretching and strengthening particular muscles have been developed. It is a good style for keeping basically fit.

Then come two Eastern disciplines, T'ai Chi and Hatha Yoga. T'ai Chi involves movement of the whole body—a very fluid, dance-like movement. Practised consistently, T'ai Chi develops physical stamina and 'grounded' body awareness, and combines this with awareness of bodily movements. Yoga seems at first sight more static since it involves special postures (or *asanas*) rather than moving exercises, but within each posture there is a complex of inner stretches, movements, and relaxations. Yoga is perhaps the most exact of the physical disciplines, combining training in bodily awareness with specific, directed exercise.

Another kind of 'exercise', the Alexander Technique, does not involve exercise, as such, at all. Like T'ai Chi and Yoga, it trains the student in awareness of the body and its movements. But it is unique in that it does so in the context of ordinary, everyday movement. Practitioners learn how best to use their body—how to re-train the bad postural habits they have acquired over years. I have not included any Alexander Technique methods here (apart from the relaxation at the end) but some people may find it well worth looking into.[2]

These four types of exercise have been chosen to demonstrate some of the basic approaches. Obviously other methods are widely practised. I should perhaps mention martial arts such as karate and aikido: from the exercise point of view, they combine different elements of the four types.

Teachers of all four methods are widely available these days. You could consider either learning one, or a little of each. Perhaps the ideal approach would be to get a thorough grounding in one physical discipline, and then learn a little of one or two others.

1. PT

(a) Ankles

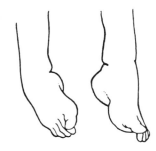

fig. 19

For strengthening and stretching ankles, try the 'Duck Walk' (fig. 19). Walk about the room—in curves, not straight lines—on the outside of your feet. Keep the feet straight. Also try lifting the toes and walking at the same time.

(b) Knees

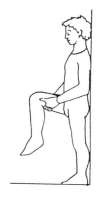

fig. 20

Knees can be gently exercised by standing against a wall and supporting one thigh at a right angle from the wall with clasped hands. Relax both ankle and knee, and then swing the lower leg (fig. 20). Rotate the lower leg only very gently, with just a very little sideways movement—swing mainly to and fro. The knee joint has very little sideways

[2]In the UK write to the Society for the Teachers of Alexander Technique at 10 London House, 266 Fulham Road, London SW10 9EL. They will send an address list of all AT teachers.

fig. 21

flexibility, and stretching it sideways too much, or too sharply, will damage it.

(c) Thighs

i. For thighs, stand on one leg near a wall (close enough so that you can reach out and regain your balance if necessary), holding one ankle with the leg bent back behind you (fig. 21). The top of the pelvis should tilt backwards, the tail-bone tuck under; the spine and chest should gently lift. Relax the thigh as you stretch it. Then repeat the exercise for the other leg.

ii. Here is a skiing exercise which is good for thighs. Stand at an arm's length, sideways, from a wall. With your hand on the wall for support, keeping the feet flat on the floor and the knees together, take the pelvis sideways towards the wall, bending the knees and arm as you go down (fig. 22). Then repeat on the other side.

fig. 22

(d) Hips and Pelvis

The hips and pelvis are often stiff and in need of opening up. These exercises especially help improve cross-legged positions. There are quite a few of them:

i. Try kneeling on all fours, knees wide apart, toes together, then with the buttocks kept low, take the chest and arms forward on the floor (fig. 23).

ii. Or kneel with one bent knee forwards, the other leg bending straight back along the floor behind you, the foot in line with the leg. Support yourself with straight arms, palms against the floor on either side of the trunk. Turn in the waist towards the kneeling leg (fig. 24).

fig. 23

iii. Again, sit cross-legged on the floor and cradle one leg in your arms, holding the knee and the sole of the foot between the elbows. Swing the leg gently from side to side. This is good for knees and thighs (fig. 25).

fig. 24

(e) Knees and Thighs

i. Lie on your back with your legs out straight. Gently bend one knee and bring it close to the body by clasping it with the hands. At the same time, keep the other straight knee on the ground (fig. 26).

ii. Squat down on the floor with your feet apart, holding the knees inside the elbows and clasped hands (fig. 27).

fig. 25 Hips/pelvis, knees, thighs

2. T'ai Chi

There are a number of very useful general exercise movements in T'ai Chi which are good for loosening and relaxing—as well as strengthening—the whole bodily framework. Here is one:

Stand with your legs a little apart, feet facing forwards. Don't stand up straight and erect, but bend slightly at the knees, let the bottom of the pelvis tuck forwards. Let the shoulders relax and the arms hang loose. Become aware of your breathing, and become particularly aware of the stomach area. Then, keeping the feet where they are for the time being, rotate the whole body from side to side, letting the arms swing freely. Let the arms lift out and swing away from the body with the centrifugal force.

fig. 26 Knees/Thighs

Swing round to the left, round to the right, turning the hips, abdomen, chest, neck, and head, all together in one fluid motion. Let the shoulders go as the arms swing. Let the loose arms fall naturally against the trunk, if need be, each time you turn. Don't turn violently, but gently and evenly: turn from the ankle.

fig. 27 Knees/Thighs

As you swing to the left, let the weight of the body move onto the right foot. As you swing right, feel the weight on the left foot. Keep the knees bent—they can be well bent now—and the lower pelvis tucked under. When you are performing the movement easily you should feel that the momentum comes only from the abdomen. After a while,

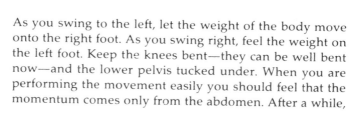

move the feet too: turn each foot on the heel when the body turns, so that, when you are three-quarters of the way to the right, the right foot comes round on the heel to follow the swing of the body. As you turn back to the front, turn the toes to the front. As you go round to the left turn on the heel to the left in the same way (fig. 28).

In spite of such a long description, this is a very simple, relaxing, and enjoyable exercise! Give it time—it may take five minutes at least to get into the feeling of it. This exercises and tones the whole body. It is especially good for the shoulders, hips, and abdomen.

fig. 28 Swinging from side to side

3. Hatha Yoga

Yoga is probably the most thorough of all the physical disciplines. There are hundreds of specific 'poses' (*asanas*) to develop every part of the body, only a few of which can be included here. The emphasis in Yoga is upon being aware of, and deliberately working, every part of the body in each pose. Inner relaxation and subtle movement is consciously 'directed' through close attention to what is happening in the body, but (as in the Alexander Technique training which follows) these subtleties can only be appreciated fully through communication with a qualified teacher.

First, here are two simple leg stretches which increase the suppleness of the leg muscles, strengthen the knees, and loosen the hip joints (figs. 29 & 30). (These are not in fact traditional Yoga exercises but are often taught in yoga classes as a 'warm-up'):

(a) Front leg stretch

Stand upright with your feet together in front of a raised ledge that is a little below waist height—this can be adjusted later according to how supple you are. Work the muscles of the thighs and knees so that the kneecaps lift up. Then, raising one leg, place one heel upon the ledge, so that the leg reaches out in front of you (do not bend the knee). The ledge should be at a height that allows you to do this

fig. 29 Front leg stretch

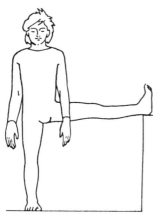

fig. 30 *Side leg stretch*

bearably, but with a good stretch. Stand erect with both feet pointing forwards, the arms relaxed at your sides. Concentrate upon what is happening in the body, directing your chest to open and the shoulders to relax back as in meditation posture. Continue to lift the leg muscles. After a while, change legs. This, and the next exercise, will develop the flexibility of the knees and the backs of the thighs very well.

(b) Sideways leg stretch

For the 'sideways leg stretch', use the same ledge as before—or a lower one if it is difficult—this time standing sideways to it. Lift one leg and place the heel on the ledge with both legs and the knees straight as before. Have the toes pointing upwards and keep the trunk in line with the standing leg. Place your hands on your hips. This is good for the hips.

(c) Triangle Pose *(Trikonasana)*

fig. 31 *Stand erect*

This pose is performed in definite stages, and each stage should be regarded as part of the pose, so that your awareness is not scattered. First stand upright with your feet together, knees and thighs lifting, hands loose at your sides. Relax your mind, concentrating and increasing your awareness of the body. Now take the feet about a metre apart, feet facing forwards. Then turn the right foot out ninety degrees to the right, and point the left foot just a little to the right. Raise both arms to shoulder height, keeping the head facing in front. Next, leading with the right arm, extend the trunk sideways over the right thigh, without bending the knee, and keeping the legs, hips, waist, and shoulders all in a straight line. Hold the calf as low down as you can while keeping that straight line. The head is still facing forwards, the knees and thighs still lifting. Next extend the left arm—wrist, hand, and fingers too—upwards to the ceiling, and turn the head, looking upwards.

fig. 32 *Legs apart, feet to side*

Remain in the pose for a few breaths, trying all the time to make it more steady. (If you can keep your awareness in

25

fig. 33 Extend over

fig. 34 Raise arm and look up

the feet and legs it will be easier to do that, and the pose will generally feel more satisfactory.) Then, keeping the knees straight, come up to the centre (on an inhalation—generally be aware of the breathing) with arms outstretched and feet facing the front. Then turn the left foot out to the left, the right foot slightly in, and (on an exhalation) extend over to the left as before.

It is a good idea to do this against a wall to keep the trunk and legs in a straight line.

Triangle pose is an excellent ail-round pose. It develops flexibility and strength in the legs, knees, hips, and lower back. Take it easy and don't strain. Do the pose twice or three times on both sides.

Triangle pose sequence:

Stand erect

Legs apart, feet to side

Extend over

Raise arm and look up

(d) Cobbler's pose *(Baddhakonasana)*

fig. 35 Cobbler's pose

Cobbler's pose is good for loosening at the hips. Sit on the floor and bring the heels together near the body, catching the feet with the hands. Sit upright with an open chest (it might be helpful to have the back against a wall). Concentrate upon the groins and thigh muscles and try to relax in the groins. As you do this the knees will move down towards the floor. Regular practice of this pose will make it easier to sit cross-legged. Two people can help one another in this pose if, as you sit against a wall, your partner kneels so that their knees hold your heels into your body. Then your partner gently places their hands upon your knees

26

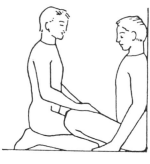

without applying pressure. Now relax in the thighs and groins. The weight of their arm will help stretch the thigh muscles slightly and give you some tension to relax into.

(e) Relaxation

It is beneficial to lie down and relax, maintaining awareness, after any session of exercise. It is especially recommended after Yoga practice. The Alexander Technique form of relaxation which follows (figs.´ 36 & 37) can be used

4. Alexander Technique

There are no specific exercises in this technique—it works through developing awareness of the body in everyday activity, like sitting, standing, and walking. But Alexander teachers do recommend the following:

(a) General relaxation

Place a few paperback books (one on top of the other) on the floor and sit down two to three feet in front of them. Bending the knees, allow your feet to rest flat on the ground about a 'shoulders' width' apart (see fig. 36). Now roll your back down on to the floor, supporting yourself with your elbows and lower arms, until you are lying on the ground with the back of your head resting on the books. Use your hands to adjust the position of the books if necessary, so that the bony back of the head is resting on the books without their touching your neck. You may need to adjust the height of the pile so that the head is neither dropping back and down towards the floor, nor raised up to the point where the chin presses down on the throat, causing discomfort. Generally, the forehead should be slightly higher than the chin.

Bring the feet a little closer to the buttocks, so that the knees balance easily as they point towards the ceiling. You may need to take the feet a little further apart or closer together to achieve this balance. A certain amount of muscle tension may be necessary to maintain this position, but it should be as little as possible so that there is no gripping on the hip joints or the toes, and no straining in the leg muscles. Slide the elbows out to the side and place your open hands on the abdomen or the hips. Let the floor support your weight.

(b) Alexander 'directions'

If the above relaxation is combined with Alexander 'directions' to the body, it will bring about a lengthening of the spine, a widening of the whole of the back, and a release and lengthening through the musculature of the legs and arms. Giving 'directions' is a process of 'thinking into the body', and is best conveyed by a teacher. Wilful attempts to make this process happen might lead to the muscles contracting further, instead of the release and integration which directing should bring about.

Alexander semi-supine position:

fig. 36 Sitting down for the relaxation

fig. 37 Final position

The directions consist in thinking of the neck muscles releasing, so that the head can move away from the shoulders in the direction shown by the arrow (in fig. 37), and in thinking of the back lengthening and widening, and of the knees releasing 'upwards' towards the ceiling away from the hip joints and the ankle joints.

After you have been lying down for some time, never get up abruptly. Rather, roll over on to one side first, letting the head lead the movement. Then get up gently.

Practised daily for 15-20 minutes, this develops greater poise, and a noticeably improved awareness of bodily movements.

28

The Windhorse symbolizes the energy of the enlightened mind carrying the Three Jewels – the Buddha, the Dharma, and the Sangha – to all sentient beings.
Buddhism is one of the fastest growing spiritual traditions in the Western world. Throughout its 2,500-year history, it has always succeeded in adapting its mode of expression to suit whatever culture it has encountered.
Windhorse Publications aims to continue this tradition as Buddhism comes to the West. Today's Westerners are heirs to the entire Buddhist tradition, free to draw instruction and inspiration from all the many schools and branches. Windhorse publishes works by authors who not only understand the Buddhist tradition but are also familiar with Western culture and the Western mind.

For orders and catalogues contact

WINDHORSE PUBLICATIONS
UNIT 1-316 THE CUSTARD FACTORY
GIBB STREET
BIRMINGHAM
B9 4AA
UK

WINDHORSE PUBLICATIONS (USA)
14 HEARTWOOD CIRCLE
NEWMARKET
NEW HAMPSHIRE
NH 03857
USA

Windhorse Publications is an arm of the Friends of the Western Buddhist Order, which has more than sixty centres on four continents. Through these centres, members of the Western Buddhist Order offer regular programmes of events for the general public and for more experienced students. These include meditation classes, public talks, study on Buddhist themes and texts, and 'bodywork' classes such as t'ai chi, yoga, and massage. The FWBO also runs several retreat centres and the Karuna Trust, a fundraising charity that supports social welfare projects in the slums and villages of India.

Many FWBO centres have residential spiritual communities and ethical businesses associated with them. Arts activities are encouraged too, as is the development of strong bonds of friendship between people who share the same ideals. In this way the FWBO is developing a unique approach to Buddhism, not simply as a set of techniques, less still as an exotic cultural interest, but as a creatively directed way of life for people living in the modern world.

If you would like more information about the FWBO please write to

LONDON BUDDHIST CENTRE
51 ROMAN ROAD
LONDON
E2 OHU
UK

ARYALOKA
HEARTWOOD CIRCLE
NEWMARKET
NEW HAMPSHIRE
NH 03857
USA

ALSO FROM WINDHORSE

KAMALASHILA
MEDITATION: THE BUDDHIST WAY OF TRANQUILLITY AND INSIGHT

A comprehensive guide to the methods and theory of meditation giving basic techniques for the beginner and detailed advice for the more experienced meditator. A practical handbook firmly grounded in Buddhist tradition but readily accessible to people with a modern Western background.
288 pages, 244 x 175, with charts and illustrations
ISBN 0 904766 56 X
Paperback £11.99/$22.99

CHRIS PAULING
INTRODUCING BUDDHISM

Chris Pauling offers a succinct answer to the question 'What is Buddhism?' in three chapters focusing on 'The Buddha', 'The Path', and 'Some History'. Now in its second and enlarged edition, *Introducing Buddhism* is a lively and engaging guide for Westerners who want to learn more about Buddhism as a path of spiritual growth. Pauling packs a lot of information into this book's pages, but also manages to convey the emotional appeal of Buddhism. He shows how this ancient wisdom is more than ever relevant to the psychological, social, and spiritual issues concerning women and men in the modern West.
80 pages
ISBN 0 904766 63 2
Paperback, £3.50/$6.50

SANGHARAKSHITA
WHO IS THE BUDDHA?

Through the centuries the Buddha has fascinated many people, but what
kind of a man was he? This book is a popular introduction to the Buddha as a
historical figure and as an archetype.
176 pages, black and white line drawings, index
ISBN 0 904766 24 1
£6.99/$11.95

SANGHARAKSHITA
A GUIDE TO THE BUDDHIST PATH

Which teachings really matter? How does one begin to practise Buddhism in
a systematic way? This is confusing territory. Without a guide one can easily
get dispirited or lost.
Like all good guides, Sangharakshita knows the terrain extremely well. At the
outset he steers us away from the dangers of sectarianism, the danger of
mistaking the part for the whole. He sorts out fact from myth, essence from
cultural accident, to reveal the fundamental teachings of Buddhism. The
result is a reliable map of the Buddhist path that anyone can follow. This is
just the guide we need and one of Windhorse Publications' best-sellers.
Part One looks at the Buddha, the Dharma (the teachings), and the Sangha
(the spiritual community). Part Two deals with a traditional formulation of
the Buddhist Path: the threefold path of Morality, Meditation, and Wisdom.
256 pages
28 illustrations, Appendices, Bibliography, Index
ISBN 0 904766 35 7
Paperback £10.95/$21.95